Who Really Said?

Famous quotes, funny quips, celebrated speakers, but . . .
who really said it?

What's **Your** Quote I.Q.?

Great Quotations Publishing Company

Compiled by Michael Ryan
Cover Art and Design by Jeff Maniglia
Typeset and Design by Julie Otlewis

© **1994** Great Quotations Publishing Company

All rights reserved.
Written permission must be secured from the publisher
to use or reproduce any part of this book,
except for brief quotations in critical reviews or articles.

Published by Great Quotations Publishing Company,
1967 Quincy Court
Glendale Heights, Illinois 60139

ISBN: 1-56245-032-8

Printed in Hong Kong

66 ———————————— 99

Famous Quotes, Funny Quips,
Immortal Words, Celebrated Speakers -
but who really said that?
Inquiring minds want to know!
Good Luck!!

This is just a test:
Who said

"Be careful about reading health books. You may die of a misprint."?

a. Mark Twain
b. Woody Allen
c. Jackie Mason

Well, to see just how much you know,
or would like to know, you will have to
turn to page 77 for the correct answers.

66 ———————————— 99

"I used to be Snow White,
but I drifted."

a. Mae West
b. Madonna
c. Phyllis Diller

"I eat dinner out three hundred sixty nights a year."

    a. Candice Bergen
    b. Woody Allen
    c. Zsa Zsa Gabor

"I never give them hell.
I just tell the truth and
they think it's hell."

    a. Ross Perot
    b. Roy Cohn
    c. Harry Truman

"It costs a lot of money
to look this cheap."

    a. Roseanne Barr
    b. Dolly Parton
    c. Mae West

"When I got out of school they retired my jersey, but it was for hygiene and sanitary reasons."

    a. George Carlin
    b. Jerry Lewis
    c. Woody Allen

"I had nothing to offer anybody except my own confusion."

    a. Jerry Lee Lewis
    b. Jack Kerouac
    c. Marlon Brando

"I find all this money a considerable burden."

a. J. Paul Getty
b. Steven Spielberg
c. Malcolm Forbes

"Nobody can make you feel inferior without your consent."

- a. Eleanor Roosevelt
- b. Winston Churchill
- c. Margaret Mead

"You can get more with a kind word
and a gun than you can
with a kind word alone."

    a. Garrison Keillor
    b. George Burns
    c. Johnny Carson

"Happiness is good health
and a bad memory."

    a. Ingrid Bergman
    b. Mark Twain
    c. Will Rogers

"Vote early and vote often."

    a. W. C. Fields
    b. Al Capone
    c. Jimmy Hoffa

"'Twas a woman who drove me to drink, and I never had the courtesy to thank her for it."

    a. George C. Scott
    b. Benny Hill
    c. W. C. Fields

"Having children is like a bowling alley installed in your brain."

    a. Martin Mull
    b. George Carlin
    c. Jerry Seinfeld

"She was so wild that when she made french toast she got her tongue caught in the toaster."

    a. Jerry Lewis
    b. Rodney Dangerfield
    c. Richard Lewis

"It's no longer a question of staying healthy. It's a question of finding a sickness you like."

a. Jackie Mason
b. Redd Foxx
c. Mark Twain

"I used to work in a
fire hydrant factory.
You couldn't park anywhere
near the place."

    a. Groucho Marx
    b. Stephen Wright
    c. Woody Allen

"I don't want any yes-men around me. I want everybody to tell me the truth even if it costs them their jobs."

    a. Samuel Goldwyn
    b. Donald Trump
    c. Richard Nixon

"Let us endeavor to live that when we die even the undertaker will be sorry."

    a. Oscar Wilde
    b. George Bernard Shaw
    c. Mark Twain

"The worst moment for the atheist is when he is really thankful and has nobody to thank."

    a. Ernie Pyle
    b. Dante Gabriel Rossetti
    c. Gore Vidal

"I'm not afraid to die.
I just don't want to be there
when it happens."

>   a. Mark Twain
>   b. Woody Allen
>   c. Bob Hope

"Marriage is a great institution,
but I'm not ready for
an institution."

    a. Joan Rivers
    b. Zsa Zsa Gabor
    c. Mae West

"Smartness runs in my family.
When I went to school I was
so smart my teacher was
in my class for five years."

    a. George Burns
    b. Fred Allen
    c. Jack Benny

" ———————————— "

"I have walked this earth for thirty years and, out of gratitude, want to leave some souvenir."

    a. Vincent van Gogh
    b. John Lennon
    c. Dylan Thomas

"Forgive your enemies,
but never forget their names."

    a. Winston Churchill
    b. Abraham Lincoln
    c. John F. Kennedy

"It is better to be unfaithful than faithful without wanting to be."

    a. Madonna
    b. Brigitte Bardot
    c. Anais Nin

"Always go to other people's funerals, otherwise they won't come to yours."

      a. Robert Morley
      b. Yogi Berra
      c. Oscar Wilde

"When angry, count four; when very angry, swear."

    a. Mark Twain
    b. Phyllis Diller
    c. Bill Cosby

"But if a man happens to find himself . . . he has a mansion which he can inhabit with dignity all the days of his life."

      a. Arnold Bennett
      b. George Bernard Shaw
      c. James Michener

"Finish each day and be done with it.
You have done what you could.
Some blunders and absurdities
no doubt crept in; forget them
as soon as you can. Tomorrow is a
new day; begin it well and serenely."

      a. Ralph Waldo Emerson
      b. Benjamin Franklin
      c. John Keats

"I'm afraid of losing my obscurity.
Genuineness only thrives
in the dark."

    a. Jerry Lee Lewis
    b. Stephen King
    c. Aldous Huxley

"Everybody is ignorant,
only on different subjects."

    a. Will Rogers
    b. Arthur Miller
    c. Thomas Hardy

"There's a time when you have to explain to your children why they're born, and it's a marvelous thing if you know the reason by then."

    a. Bill Cosby
    b. Randall Jarrell
    c. Hazel Scott

"If you can't laugh at yourself, make fun of other people."

    a. Bobby Slaton
    b. Garrison Keillor
    c. Mel Brooks

"I believe that the power to
make money is a gift from God."

    a. Malcolm Forbes
    b. Nelson Rockefeller
    c. Joseph Kennedy

"I often quote myself.
It adds spice to my conversation."

    a. Edward Young
    b. H.W. Fowler
    c. George Bernard Shaw

"The greatest lesson in life
is to know that fools
are right sometimes."

    a. Winston Churchill
    b. Bertrand Russell
    c. Blaise Pascal

"One of my problems is that
I internalize everything.
I can't express anger;
I grow a tumor instead.

    a. George Burns
    b. Woody Allen
    c. Jack Benny

"I've never been drunk,
but often I've been overserved."

        a. George Gobel
        b. Phil Harris
        c. F. Scott Fitzgerald

"Only love interests me, and I am only in contact with things that revolve around love.

    a. Marilyn Monroe
    b. Casanova
    c. Marc Chagall

"Being entirely honest with oneself
is a good exercise."

      a. Sigmund Freud
      b. Ralph Waldo Emerson
      c. Mark Twain

"Beauty is an ecstasy;
it is as simple as hunger.
There is really nothing to
be said about it."

    a. Gustave Flaubert
    b. John Keats
    c. W. Somerset Maugham

"When one door of happiness closes, another opens; but often we look so long at the closed door that we do not see the one which has been opened for us.

        a. Ayn Rand
        b. Robert Frost
        c. Helen Keller

"Miracles happen to those
that believe in them."

    a. Bill Cosby
    b. Bernard Berenson
    c. Charles Lamb

"Two persons must believe in
each other, and feel that it
can be done and must be done;
in that way they are enormously
strong. They must keep up
each others courage."

        a. Vincent van Gogh
        b. Robert H. Schuller
        c. Dr. Wayne Dyer

"In the long run men only hit what they aim at. Therefore, though they should fail immediately, they had better aim at something high."

    a. Charles Simmons
    b. Sigmund Freud
    c. Henry David Thoreau

"Believe in dreams.
Never believe in hurts . . .
You can't let the grief
and the hurts and the
breaking experiences of life
control your future decisions."

      a. Scott Peck
      b. Robert Schuller
      c. Bertrand Russell

"Life is an unanswered question, but let's still believe in the dignity and importance of the question."

    a. Tennessee Williams
    b. Kurt Vonnegut
    c. John Keats

" "

"I'm living so far beyond
my income that we may almost
be said to be living apart."

      a. e e cummings
      b. Will Rogers
      c. W.C. Fields

"You don't have to deserve your mother's love. You have to deserve your father's. He's more particular."

       a. Alvin Toffler
       b. Robert Frost
       c. Josh Billings

"Once you say you're going to settle for second, that's what happens to you in life, I find."

    a. John F. Kennedy
    b. Vince Lombardi
    c. Franklin D. Roosevelt

"He has all the virtues I dislike and none of the vices I admire."

    a. John F. Kennedy
    b. Vince Lombardi
    c. Franklin D. Roosevelt

"There is only one thing about which I am certain, and that is that there is very little about which one can be certain."

    a. W. Somerset Maugham
    b. Albert Camus
    c. Mark Twain

"The world is a madhouse, so it's only right that it is patrolled by armed idiots."

    a. Bernard Berenson
    b. Brendan Behan
    c. George Price

"Never argue with people who buy ink by the gallon."

    a. Fred Allen
    b. Bobby Slayton
    c. Tommy Lasorda

"What luck for rulers that men do not think."

    a. Adolf Hitler
    b. Napoleon Bonaparte
    c. Abraham Lincoln

"I can live for two months
on a good compliment."

    a. Samuel Butler
    b. Mark Twain
    c. Ogden Nash

"Pessimist - one who, when he has the choice of two evils, chooses both."

    a. William Butler Yeats
    b. Robert Alden
    c. Oscar Wilde

"I generally avoid temptation unless I can't resist it."

    a. Art Buchwald
    b. Mae West
    c. W.C. Fields

"I am as bad as the worst, but, thank God, I am as good as the best."

    a. Walt Whitman
    b. George Will
    c. Mickey Rooney

"The only unnatural sexual behavior is none at all."

   a. Sigmund Freud
   b. Alex Comfort
   c. John Lennon

"Start every day off with a smile
and get it over with."

    a. George Burns
    b. W. C. Fields
    c. Kurt Vonnegut, Jr.

"The man with the best job in the country is the Vice President. All he has to do is get up every morning and say, 'How's the President?'"

    a. H.L. Mencken
    b. Mort Sahl
    c. Will Rogers

"When we talk to God, we're praying.
When God talks to us,
we're schizophrenic."

    a. Phyllis Diller
    b. Lily Tomlin
    c. Lenny Bruce

"We should take care not to
make the intellect our god;
it has, of course, powerful muscles,
but no personality."

> a. Albert Einstein
> b. John Keats
> c. Sigmund Freud

"The significance of a man is not what he attains but rather in what he longs to attain."

    a. Winston Churchill
    b. Kahil Gibran
    c. Goethe

"The public is wonderfully tolerant.
It forgives everything except genius."

      a. William Blake
      b. James Russel Lowell
      c. Oscar Wilde

"Experience teaches only
the teachable."

    a. Aldous Huxley
    b. Henry Geaye
    c. Henry Kissinger

" Destiny is what you are supposed to do in life. Fate is what kicks you in the ass to make you do it."

    a. Henry Miller
    b. Vince Lombardi
    c. Dwight D. Eisenhower

"Only two things are necessary to
keep one's wife happy.
One is to let her think she is
having her own way,
and the other, to let her have it."

        a. Saul Bellow
        b. Lyndon B. Johnson
        c. Mark Twain

"My problem lies in reconciling
my gross habits with
my net income."

    a. Errol Flynn
    b. Jackie Mason
    c. Richard Burton

"More than any time in history
mankind faces a crossroads.
One path leads to dispair and
utter hopelessness, the other
to total extinction.
Let us pray that we have
the wisdom to choose correctly."

    a. George Bernard Shaw
    b. Woody Allen
    c. Steve Martin

"When I was a boy I was told that anybody could become president; I'm beginning to believe it."

    a. Clarence Darrow
    b. William F. Buckley, Jr.
    c. Johnny Carson

"Find joy in simplicity, self respect, and indifference to what lies between virtue and vice.
Love the human race.
Follow the divine."

    a. Thomas Fuller
    b. Marcus Aurelius
    c. Oscar Wilde

"─────99

"The only beautiful things are the things that do not concern us."

    a. John Keats
    b. Oscar Wilde
    c. William Blake

"Learn to value yourself,
which means:
To fight for your happiness."

    a. Benjamin Franklin
    b. Fyodor Dostoevsky
    c. Ayn Rand

Answers

Test - a	24. a	47. b	70. b
2. a	25. c	48. a	71. a
3. b	26. b	49. a	72. b
4. c	27. b	50. b	73. a
5. b	28. a	51. a	74. b
6. a	29. c	52. c	75. b
7. b	30. a	53. a	76. c
8. a	31. c	54. b	
9. a	32. a	55. c	
10. c	33. c	56. a	
11. a	34. a	57. b	
12. b	35. b	58. c	
13. c	36. c	59. b	
14. a	37. a	60. a	
15. b	38. b	61. a	
16. a	39. a	62. b	
17. b	40. c	63. c	
18. a	41. a	64. b	
19. c	42. c	65. a	
20. b	43. c	66. b	
21. b	44. b	67. c	
22. c	45. a	68. a	
23. a	46. c	69. a	

We hope you have enjoyed this book! We welcome your comments and suggestions. Please send any ideas you may have to the attention of our
New Product Department

—The Editor

Other Titles by Great Quotations Publishing Company
COMB BOUND

- A Friend Is
- A Smile Increases Your Face Value
- Aged to Perfection
- An Apple A Day
- Backfield in Motion
- Batter Up
- Bedside Manner
- Believe and Achieve
- Best in Business Humor
- Birthday Wishes
- Books Are Better
- Boyfriends Live Longer Than Husbands
- Change Your Thoughts, Change Your Life
- Don't Marry, Be Happy
- Double Dribble
- Golf Humor
- Graduation - Keys To Success
- Great Quotes - Great Comedians
- Halfway Home (Surviving the Middle Years)
- Harvest Of THoughts
- Inspirations
- Joy Of Family
- Keys To Happiness
- Life's Winning Tips
- Love, Honor, Cherish
- Love, Sex & Marriage
- Love On Your Wedding Day
- Mothers And Babies
- Never Give Up
- Our Life Together
- Over The Hill Sex
- Political Humor
- Quotations from African-American
- Real Friends
- Retirement
- Sports Poop
- Sports Quotes
- Stress
- Teachers Inspirations
- Thank You
- The Quest For Success
- Things You'll Learn
- Thinking Of You
- Thoughts From The Heart
- To A Very Special Daughter
- To A Very Special Son
- To A Very Special Grandparent
- To A Very Special Love
- To My Mother
- To My Father
- Unofficial Christmas Survival Guide
- Unofficial Executive Survival Guide
- Unofficial Stress Test
- Unofficial Survival Guide to Parenthood
- Unofficial Vacation Guide
- Ordinary Men, Extraordinary Lives
- Our Thoughts Are Prayers
- What To Tell Your Children
- Who Really Said
- Wonders & Joys Of Christmas
- Words From Great Women

PAPERBACK

- 199 Useful Things to Do With A Politician
- 201 Best Things Ever Said
- A Lifetime of Love
- A Light Heart Lives Long
- A Teacher Is Better Than Two Books
- As A Cat Thinketh
- Cheatnotes On Life
- Chicken Soup
- Dear Mr. President
- Father Knows Best
- Food For Thought
- Golden Years/Golden Words
- Happiness Walks On Busy Feet
- Heal The World
- Hooked on Golf
- Hollywords
- I'm Not Over The Hill
- In Celebration of Women
- Life's Simple Pleasures
- Mother - A Bouquet of Love
- Motivation Magic
- Mrs. Webster's Dictionary
- Reflections
- Romantic Rendezvous
- Sports Page
- So Many Ways To Say Thank You
- The ABC's of Parenting
- The Best Of Friends
- The Birthday Astrologer
- The Little Book of Spiritual Wisdom
- Things You'll Learn, If You Live Long Enough

PERPETUAL CALENDARS

Apple A Day
Country Proverbs
Each Day A New Beginning
Friends Forever
Golf Forever
Home Is Where The Heart Is
Proverbs
Seasonings
Simply The Best Dad
Simple The Best Mom
Simple Ways To Say I Love You
Teacher"s" Are "First Class!"

Great Quotations Publishing Company

1967 Quincy Court
Glendale Heights, IL 60139-2045
Phone (708) 582-2800
FAX (708) 582-2813